WHY COLORED PEOPLE

IN

PHILADELPHIA

ARE

EXCLUDED FROM THE STREET CARS.

PHILADELPHIA:
MERRIHEW & SON, PRINTERS,
No. 243 Arch Street, below Third St.
1866.

THE COLORED PEOPLE AND THE CARS.

Some remarks lately communicated to the New York Anti-Slavery Standard, on the continued exclusion of colored people from our street cars, leave the impression that no efforts have been made here to procure for this class of people admission to these cars. This is incorrect. It will be found on inquiry, that a Committee, consisting of some twenty-five or thirty gentlemen, appointed at a public meeting, in January of last year, to effect, if possible, this object, is still in existence. This Committee is evidently somewhat slow. No report of its proceedings has yet been published, and the only reason suggested for its silence is, that there has been nothing good to report: an insufficient reason.

But these gentlemen have not been entirely idle. It seems that immediately on their appointment, they called on the respective Presidents of the nineteen street railway companies, and, in a courteous manner, requested them to withdraw from their list of running regulations the rule excluding colored people. Some few favored compliance, more or less conditional, the others not; but all, or nearly all, finally settled on the subterfuge of referring the question to a car-vote of their passengers. The subterfuge answered its purpose, for the self-respecting part of the community did not vote.

Shortly after this vote was taken, a colored man was ejected from a car by the help of a policeman. The Committee called on the late Mayor Henry, and respectfully inquired if this had been done by his order. His reply was: "Not by my order, but with my knowledge and approbation; as the right to exclude colored people has been claimed by the railway companies, and has not been judicially determined, the police assists in maintaining the rules of the companies, to prevent breaches of the peace." And he added: "I am not with you, gentlemen; I do not wish the ladies of my family to ride in the cars with colored people." It is proper to state here, that at the time of this interview, the latest three decisions of the Courts of the country, bearing on this question, had been directly against the right of exclusion, —the last being that of Judge Allison, of our Court of Quarter Sessions.

The Committee then turned to the Legislature. A bill to prevent exclusion from the cars on account of race or color had been introduced into, and passed by the Senate, early in the session of 1865, and was referred to the Passenger Railway Committee of the House. Here it was smothered. No persuasion could induce this Railway Committee,—twelve out of its fifteen members being Republicans, and eight, Republicans from Philadelphia,—to report the bill to the House in any shape. According to the statement of the Chairman, Mr. Lee, the school-boy trick was resorted to of stealing it from his file, in order that it might be said that there was no such bill in the hands of the Committee. This assertion was made to an inquirer, several times over, by Mr. Freeborn, one of its members.

Finally, recourse was had to the Courts. Funds were raised, and within the last sixteen months, the Committee has attempted to bring suits for assault in seven different cases of ejection, all of which have been ignored by various grand juries,—the last only a few days ago. In one case, a white man,—a highly respectable physician,—who interposed, by remonstrance only, to prevent the ejection of a colored man, was himself ejected. He brought an action for assault, and his complaint was ignored also. In five of these cases civil actions for damages have been commenced, which are still pending. One of them, by appeal from a verdict, given under a charge of Judge Thompson, in Nisi Prius, against the ejected plaintiff, is now on its way to the Supreme Court in banc, where it is hoped the whole question will be finally and justly settled.

The colored people at present rarely make any attempt to enter the cars. As is their wont, they submit peaceably to what they must. The last case of ejection was that of a young woman, so light of color that she was mistaken for white, and invited into a car of the Union Line by its conductor. When he found she was colored, he ejected her with violence, and somewhat to her personal injury.

Thus stands this matter at present; and such has been the action of official bodies in it. Let us now see what has been the action of the unofficial public, and what spirit that public has manifested towards it indirectly, by its action on kindred matters. The claim of the colored people to enter the cars, though a local question, is inseparable from the great policy of Equality before the Law, now offering itself to the national acceptance; and any local fact which bears on the one relates also to the other, and is therefore relevant to this subject.

And first, it is found that even colored women, when ejected from the cars with insult and violence, seldom meet with sympathy from the casual white passengers, of either sex, who are present, while the conductor often finds active partisans among them. But one white passenger has ever volunteered testimony in any case; and for want of this, generally the only proof possible, several cases have been dropped.

Events early last year, such as the voting in the cars, the petition of the men working at the Navy Yard for continued exclusion of colored people on the Second and Third Street Line, the "fillibustering" of several hundred women, employed by the Government on army clothing, to defeat the Fifth and Sixth Street experiment of admission, and other acts of violence, show clearly that the classes represented by these men and women are bitterly opposed to admission.

Of our seven daily newspapers, two—the *Press* and *Bulletin*—have spoken out manfully and repeatedly in reproof of these outrages and in defence of the rights of the colored people. The others, it is believed, while admitting communications on both sides, have been editorially silent on the subject. In their local items, however, they have generally given a version of these disturbances unfavorable to the ejected colored people, under the heading of "riotous conduct of negroes," or some similar caption.

Grand juries, from the way in which their members are brought together, may be supposed fairly to represent the average public sentiment on this question, and their uniform action has been shown. Colored children have never been admitted to our general public schools, and the Associated Friends of the Freedmen in this city, who have lately adopted, as one of their cardinal rules, the admission of children of both colors, indiscriminately, to their schools in the South, consider that any effort to introduce the same rule here would be vain.

Only three members—Generals Owen, Tyndale, and Collis—of the Military Committee of Arrangements of sixteen, for the late celebration of the Fourth of July in this city, favored inviting colored troops to join in it; and the officers of the "California" Regiment (71st P. V.) gave notice, that if such troops did parade, their regiment must decline to do so, and would forward its colors to Harrisburg by express.

On the 30th of June last there were, distributed through sixteen counties of the State, and supported by State appropriations amounting in all to $525,000, twenty-nine School-Homes, three being in this city, containing 1837 orphans of white soldiers; and, according to the estimate of the Superintendent, by the 1st of December next, the number is expected to reach 3000. But, after careful inquiry, it does not appear that an orphan child of any one of the 1488 colored soldiers who lost their lives in the service, out of the 8681 belonging, according to official records, to Pennsylvania, and enlisted at Camp Wm. Penn, has yet found its way into any of these schools, or been provided for in any manner out of the above fund. You examine the Act, and find nothing there to exclude them from these privileges; you ask explanation of the school matrons, and are told that they never before heard the thing mentioned; and in reading the two annual reports of the Superintendent, Mr. Thomas H. Burrows, you find not a word implying knowledge of the fact that there was a single colored soldier enlisted in the State. Now on the 6th of July, 1863, at National Hall, the Hon. Wm. D. Kelley, a member of the late Supervisory Committee for Recruiting Colored Regiments, in presence of his colleagues and a large concourse of people, white and colored, asked, addressing his colored auditors: "Will you not spring to arms, and march to the higher destiny which awaits your race?" Then turning to his colleagues and their white friends, he asked: "Will you not see that their orphans are secured such educational opportunities as a great and humane commonwealth should provide for the orphans of patriots?" Both these appeals were answered by loud shouts of assent. And the men of color did "spring to arms," and marched—not exactly "to the higher destiny which awaits their race," for that seems to be rather a long march. They, however, kept their pledge; the country admits that. But, Men of the late Supervisory Committee, and the thousands whom you represented, how have you kept yours?

Again: at the corner of Sixteenth and Filbert Streets, in this city, there is a most comfortable Home for Disabled Soldiers. The State, thus far, has appropriated $5000 a year and the rent of the building to its support; the balance of its fund, $115,000, is chiefly the proceeds of a fair held last October at the Academy of Music for the benefit of disabled soldiers without regard to color. Colored disabled soldiers are of course admitted to this institution, as well as white, and both receive the same kind of fare. But the 160 white inmates eat, sleep, amuse themselves, and attend the four schools of different grades, under hired teachers, in well-aired and well-lighted rooms, distributed through the high main building, separate things, for them, being kept separate. The seven colored disabled soldiers (enlisted at Camp William Penn) are quartered in a frame appendage to this establishment, built on the pavement of the back yard, to which their privileges are mainly restricted; and here they receive gratuitous lessons from their benevolent volunteer teacher, Miss Biddle. There is still room in this Home for one hundred more white soldiers, but there are present accommodations for no more who are colored. An applicant, formerly of the 1st U. S. C. T., wounded in the hand, lately requested to be allowed quarters there for a day or two, until he could get work, and was told that the colored ward was full. Another colored soldier, his regiment not known, but who had lost an arm in the service, was also lately turned away for the same reason. To the inquiry whether it is absolutely necessary to make the distinction above noted, the prompt answer is, "Yes; for otherwise the white soldiers would make a row." But according to all testimony received, the white soldiers most cheerfully accorded the post of danger, during the late war, to the enlisted Blacks; and that the latter as cheerfully accepted and bravely maintained this post, many battle-fields—Fort Wagner, Port Hudson and Petersburg among the rest—testify. And it would seem that this fact might be used as an unanswerable reason for establishing equality of privilege in quarters where these soldiers meet in time of peace. The quarters being free of expense to all, those who might dislike the conditions could be made free to leave them. But it is found that this suggestion, when made, cannot be entertained for a moment.

Now let us look at the question in its political aspect. And attention may be called first to the fact that several members of the late House Passenger Railway Committee,—the gentlemen who, in their quality of legislative abortionists, prevented the anti-exclusion bill from seeing the light,—were returned to the Legislature at the last Fall election, by a full party vote, although this transaction had been fully made known through the newspapers. This shows clearly that, by their course in regard to the rights of the colored people, they had not forfeited the confidence of our so-called radicals. One of these gentlemen, the same who reiterated the assertion that "there was no such bill in the hands of the Committee," is reputed to be one of the most respectable and useful members of the Philadelphia delegation. He is an especial favorite of the Union League, of which he has become a member since his services on the above Committee were rendered, and he was lately the recipient of a complimentary gift, with appropriate ceremonials, in one of its rooms, as a token of his legislative merit. This incident is mentioned only because it serves to show what manner of spirit the League is of, in regard to this question of admission; and one is constrained to believe that this spirit partakes largely of indifference, tinged with contempt, and therefore of inert opposition. And if anything were wanting to confirm this impression, it is to be found in the fact that the League declines to permit the rare distributing powers of its Publication Committee to be used in spreading over the State documents which distinctly advocate negro suffrage.

Next, it will be remembered how, last Fall, all classes of Republicans, from the most conservative to, with few exceptions, the most radical, united in expressions of the sincerest regret that the late Mayor Henry positively declined again to be their candidate. Now it is the general belief of those who have all along taken an interest in this matter, that, with the assistance of the Mayor, our colored people could have gained full admission to the cars more than eighteen months ago, just as similar admission was obtained for the colored people of New York, through the energetic course adopted in their favor by Police Commissioner Ecton. There was then a sort of factitious public feeling still running in favor of colored folks; war-made abolitionism had not all melted away; peace had not come, and we might need more of them to fight for us; these facts had their effect on the public mind, and were reflected on the Board of Presidents; the Fifth and Sixth Street Company tried the experiment of admission for a month; their whole line was beginning to waver, when just then the Mayor stepped to their side with his powerful official influence and aid, and turned the scale in their favor. In their battle with the car-invading negroes, he was their needle-gun. And yet, with a full knowledge of these facts, no one doubts that the Republicans, last October, would gladly have re-elected Mr. Henry as their Mayor, and that by a larger majority than he ever before received. And it must be admitted that the late Mayor is a most respectable man. By almost universal consent, he was as brave and incorruptible in office as he has always been pure in morals and unaffected in piety in private life. Possibly, here and there an extremist might be found to object, that, thus openly to set up, as he did, his own prejudices and those of his family, in the place of law, justice and humanity, as his rule of official conduct, to the manifest injury of twenty-seven thousands of innocent people, was a most shameless abuse of power and perversion of authority. But this objection, with the word shameless, cannot be admitted except "with a difference." A young child, rolling upon the carpet and freely exposing its little person, no one calls shameless; it is simply unconscious. Just so was the late Mayor Henry. Many great and good men have done gross wrongs unconsciously. Paul, when he was "haling men and women," very much as our policemen were permitted to do last year, and with purposes not dissimilar, since both were actuated by the spirit of persecution, "verily thought" that he "ought to do" these things; though it is true, at that time, Paul did not pretend to be a Christian. We may, however, rest assured that when by such an inverted arrangement of the moral forces as is described above, only negroes are brought within the official vice and made to feel sharp pressure, neither the late Mayor, nor the great majority of his friends and supporters, see the matter in any discreditable light. And it may as well be confessed, once for all, that to treat a man's sentiments in respect to negroes as of any importance, in making up your estimate of his character; or to announce, as your own motive, in whatever you may do for colored people, the simple desire to do them good, because it is just, irrespective of any object beyond, such as to save white recruits, to weaken an enemy, or to gain possible future votes,—is to bring upon yourself the contempt, secret or open, strong or mild, of nine-tenths of the people you meet.

When Mr. Charles Gibbons, in his stirring address to the Union League, shortly after the murder of Mr. Lincoln, described this murder and other crimes of the South as "representative acts of slavery," and logically referred to the wrongs done to the colored people in this city in the same connection, the conclusion of his address was pronounced "anti-climax." "After electrifying his audience," it was said, "he flatted right down to the small matter of the cars and colored people." Now while anything relating to the final position in this country of four millions of its people, a question which has already caused one war, and which may cause another, is contemptuously termed "small" by highly intelligent and influential men, we have much to learn and much to suffer before this question can be settled.

Another class indication of public feeling on this subject must not be passed by in silence. At a late series of large and excited meetings of our clergy and laity convened to remonstrate against the running of the street cars on Sunday, not a word was said by the remonstrants, though their attention was called to the matter, against the exclusion of colored people from these cars on week-days. Like the grand juries, they ignored the subject. Further, it is believed that only three of the white clergy of this city have spoken, either from pulpit or platform, in reprobation of this gross wrong; and if there are cases in which saying nothing is committing sin, this would seem to be one of them. But fair and reasonable men are tired of hearing clergymen berated for not doing that which, if they would still remain clergymen, they cannot do. It is easy and safe for a pastor to lay before his people a certain set of what may be called sins by common consent, such as over-worldliness, inattention to religion and the like. One portion of his hearers meekly bows to this reproof, and the remainder tacitly accepts it without argument. But when he earnestly calls on them to give up some darling sin, which they hug to their bosoms because they do not admit that it is such, his relations to them are apt, at once, to become such as were those of St. Paul to the beasts of Ephesus. And to expect a pastor fiercely to throttle each living, vigorous, but unconfessed, if not unconscious sin of his people, as it comes up, for $400 a year, (the average clerical pay, it is said, of the wealthiest sect in this State,) and then to lose this small stipend, which he is likely to do by dismissal, as the result of the conflict, is asking more than a fair day's work for less than a fair day's wages. Here and there may be found a man who can afford to enter into this fight. One, rich in natural gifts, holds his hearers by the power of personal magnetism, while he pours into their ears a torrent of unwelcome truths, to which they listen, like the Wedding Guest, because they "cannot choose but hear," and then, not a few go away, like an awakened medium, uninfluenced by them. Another, whose voice neither denouncement nor desertion can silence, or make falter, because its words are but the imperative utterances of a great heart ever flowing in full tide, with good will to man, simply as man, always finds fit audience though few. But these are exceptions, and though courage might add to them, the great body of our clergymen must preach what their people are not unwilling to hear, or cease to earn bread for their families as clergymen. And here is the true reason of their silence, or hesitating speech, on such proposed subjects of reform as, at the time, have found but small acceptance; and as men and things go, this reason is sufficient. Their grave fault is that they keep it shut up in that dark, back cell of the heart, to which men never admit each other, and rarely themselves, and put forward such phrases as "secular subjects," "politics in the pulpit," and (a profanation of the Holy Word) "my kingdom is not of this world," in the place of it. Hence the chronic false position in which they stand to society. For from the very nature of their relations either to their people, an aristocracy, or their own order, the clergy are everywhere conservative and not progressive. When Luther began to be a reformer he ceased to be a monk. All that can reasonably be expected of them is not to break new soil, but to refrain from upholding old abuses, and (a most important trust) carefully to keep in order in the old way, but with a readiness to accept new principles and improved methods, the ground already fenced in. Their true type of reform is that of Mr. Lincoln. He never professed to move except at the word of the people, but he always watched for and joyfully obeyed the first sure signal to advance. But there are cases in which clergymen are called on to make a direct attack on a social abuse, and in which the practical good sense of all classes will uphold them in so doing, whether that abuse has general countenance or not; and that is where the defence of their own order demands it. Such a supposed demand was the true cause of their late loud and unwise protest against the running of the cars on Sunday. They mistakenly believed this movement to be an invasion of their special domain, which it was their duty to repel; whereas, if permitted, it would unquestionably here, as it has done elsewhere, not only benefit the poor, but increase church-going. And yet, notwithstanding this readiness to rally in general self-defence, it appears that when the Rev. Mr. Allston, rector of St. Thomas' (Colored Episcopal) Church, was expelled from a Lombard and South Street car, and in such a manner that the strength of his hands alone kept his head from being dashed on the pavement, some of his brethren simply offered to see that any expense which he might incur in case he chose to prosecute, should be made up to him. One feels inclined to ask these gentlemen if they would have contented themselves with this, as sufficient action in the case, had the rector of Christ Church, or of St. Luke's, or even so young a man as the rector of Holy

Trinity, been subjected to such an outrage as this,—one at any time likely to be repeated, and which is, in fact, regularly kept up by continued exclusion. There can hardly be a doubt that, had this been the case of a white clergyman, a meeting would have been called, a protest made, and a deputation, lay and clerical, appointed to wait on Mr. Dropsie, the President of the company, or some other vigorous measures taken, to exact redress for present, and guarantees against future injuries. This would be due, not only to the outraged brother, but to themselves, outraged in him. The preservation of their influence with, and the respect in which it is necessary they should be held by, society, would imperatively demand such a course ; and the only conceivable reason why it was not pursued in the case of the Rev. Mr. Allston is, that except by a sort of ecclesiastical fiction, the Episcopal clergy of Philadelphia do not consider him of their order, nor feel that, in the eyes of this community, their reputation is in any manner identified with his ; and therefore it was not necessary to their common interests that they should pursue it.

But there is a symptom of public opinion on this subject worse than the foregoing. The very Committee appointed for the special purpose of securing to the colored people their rights, failed to be true to their trust when tried by the test of party politics. At a meeting of the said Committee, held not long before the last municipal election, a resolution was offered, the purport of which was, to ask of the present Mayor, when a candidate, a statement in writing as to the course he intended to pursue in regard to this question, if elected. But the Committee deprecated the very thought of jeopardizing the success of the Republican candidate, by a committal on such a question as this. The resolution was voted down by a majority of more than ten to one of the members present. This action is to be regretted, not only on account of its immediate effect on the work in hand,—for it was of course reported to the Board of Presidents, who naturally concluded that the Committee was not in earnest,—but because it established the fact of weakness in that part of society in which, of late, we have most looked for strength ; and that is in the part which consists of our able and leading private men of business. If it is true of clergymen that they cannot be our leaders in reform, it is no less so of politicians, even of the best class, in or out of office, and of professional philanthropists, and of managers of the various bodies of benevolent men and women permanently organized for particular purposes relating to the public good. All these are, or in time will be, biassed, either consciously or unconsciously, by private interests, or party ties, or special objects in connection with these Associations, whose plans they will seek to shape with a view to their own purposes. But there is another disqualification common to them all. They are not independent. They have somebody to consult besides themselves. They do not act directly from their own convictions, but are constantly striving to ascertain the average conviction of the public, or of their constituents, in order to act from that; and as each of their constituents, to a degree, is independent, and therefore gives fair play to his convictions, they are very apt to under-estimate this average, and fall short of it in action: Or, as Wendell Phillips tersely states it, "representatives are timid, principals are bold." Successful private men of business are free from these entanglements and temptations; they alone, as a class, can afford to disregard them, and therefore they and no others are fitted to take the lead in, or be the chief promoters of, new movements for the good of society. The best of this class are earnest, liberal, intelligent, brief in discussion, practical and direct in operation, regardless of official honors and the gains connected therewith, and, above all, they know how to master and use wealth, without being in turn mastered by it. The danger of such men is not in imprudence; the difficulty is to find quite enough of them who are not too prudent; and if there are some working with them who are earnest even to bitterness, and have nothing which they greatly fear to lose, or hope to gain,—not even reputation,—so that uses are performed, truths told and justice satisfied, it will be all the better. Not the least valuable effect of the late war was the discovery which it made for us of the great wealth of the country in this kind of men. A few such men, in spite of the covert contempt and inert opposition of President, Cabinet, congressmen, generals, and army surgeons, made the Sanitary Commission an institution, whose great and business-like work of patriotic charity and mercy became the admiration of the civilized world. They first made the necessity and practicability of their plan clear to the people, and then, with them at their back, forced an unwilling government to recognize and accept the Commission as a power to do good. Similar in character and results was the Christian Commission, in the President of which is found the most eminent single example that the war afforded, in support of this position; such, also, but more limited in their operations, because less popular, are the Freedmen's Associations; and such, in its original conception and working during the war, was the Union League.

The men who led in these movements did not go to politicians and ask if their plans were expedient, party interests considered. But with the desire to do good for their motive and their own native energies for their power, success soon brought the politicians to them. And if private men, or associations of private men, will, this may always be the case. To this end they have but to accept, and act up to these propositions: That this country, with such a people in it as carried through the late war, can never be ruined, politicians to the contrary notwithstanding; that its nearest approach to ruin will come from temporizing; that party management never saved a country nor advanced a just cause; that a country is saved and a just cause advanced only by doing justice and cultivating a right public opinion; that power on any other basis is better lost than kept, even when the party that gains is worse than the party that loses it; that when legitimate means fail, or have not been used, to form this basis by a party in power, then the misdeeds of evil men in power are the only resource left to the country for creating a public opinion against their own evil policy and in favor of justice, which they will do by causing reaction; that this is the chief use of, and necessity for, a second party in the State, and that these propositions are good at all times and in every crisis, not excepting the present. By taking a firm stand on this ground, and refusing absolutely to support for office candidates of inadequate ability, bad personal character, or doubtful firmness of principle, private men may become a power in the State, instead of remaining the mere voting machines which they are at present in the hands of cunning, short-sighted and selfish politicians. The chief political value of such private men, in their associated capacity, and the special advantage they possess over all other bodies convened for consultation with a view to the public good, consist in their being free to discuss and advocate just measures, with simple directness and without side issues, and in their ability to enlighten, advance and fortify public opinion in respect to these measures. When they do this, they furnish to representative bodies—what they most need—firm and well cleared ground to stand and work upon. But they never can do this as mere appendages of State Central Committees, nor if, while they are free from the representative responsibilities of congressmen, they are more timid than Congress and speak only in echo of it, and long after it. And whether they act as political or social reformers, there must be no distrust of justice, as always a safe guide, and no putting her aside for the lead of party hacks, as was unfortunately the case with the aforesaid Car Committee; and the colored people, when they saw their chosen champions thus postpone justice, in their case, to party expediency, might well ask where they were to look for any real support in this demand for their simple rights.

Aside then from the action of official and conventional bodies, it has been shown that large numbers of the laboring classes are opposed to the unreserved use of the cars by the colored people; and it must be inferred from the foregoing facts that but a small number of any class earnestly and actively advocate it. Between these extremes is the great body of the respectable, intelligent and influential portion of the community, the members of which are generally self-restraining and above violence in speech or act, and who, at first sight, one might suppose to be indifferent on the question, or perhaps torpidly in favor of admission. A little friction, however, brings to the surface unmistakable evidence that this body also is permeated with latent prejudice sufficient to carry it, imperceptibly perhaps and by dead weight only, but still to carry it against the colored people. Many belong to this class who would take offence if told so. It is not hard to find old hereditary abolitionists—Orthodox and other Friends, and members of the late Supervisory Committee for Recruiting Colored

Regiments, who coldly decline all overtures for coöperation in this work. The abolition of Slavery away in the South was all very well, but here is a matter of personal contact. They are not opposed, themselves, to riding with colored people—certainly not. The colored people may get into the cars if they can; they will not hinder it. But they do wish there were baths furnished at the public expense, for the use of these friends, in order that they might be made thereby less offensive to ladies. And from these ladies, no doubt, comes an opposition—indirect and partially concealed—apparent perhaps only through the manner and tone of the father, husband or brother, but still most obstinate. It is often curious to observe how the discussion of this subject will set in motion two opposing moral currents in the same religious and cultivated female mind; that of conscience, which calls for the admission of the colored people, and that of prejudice, which hopes they will not get it. And thus the moral nature of many men and women, who in general are friendly to equal rights, on this question is divided. The sense of justice not being quickened by sympathy, their movements in respect to it are like those of a man palsied on one side—hindering rather than helpful. And it is this great, respectable and intelligent portion of the community that is really responsible for these wrongs and disturbances.

John Swift, a hard, shrewd man, now gone to his place, but in 1838 Mayor of this city, told a committee of Friends who called on him, on the 17th of May of that year, for protection against men who threatened violence, that "public opinion makes mobs;" and on the same night a mob, so made, after a short, mild speech from the said Mayor, counselling order and stating that the military would not be called out, burnt down Pennsylvania Hall. And every mob that the country has seen, during the last century, has had a similar origin and support, from that of the Paxton Boys against harmless Indians, in 1763, encouraged up to the threshhold of murder, and then only opposed, when too late, by the Rev. Mr. Elder and his colleagues, to that of the New York Irish rioters against the negroes and the draft, in 1863, that was addressed as "my friends" by

Gov. Seymour, the representative of a great party. And, to bring this subject up to date, may be added the late rebel mob at New Orleans, hissed on, in its wholesale work of murder, by the President of the United States through the telegraph. The brain does not more surely impel or restrain the hand, than do the more educated and influential classes, however imperceptibly, those that are less so, in all cases in which premeditated violence is forseen. And had there really existed any considerable degree of this moral restraining power in our community, these outrages against the people of color would long since have ceased.

We are forced then to the conclusion that this community, as a body, by long indulgence in the wicked habit of wronging and maltreating colored people, has become, like a moral lunatic, utterly powerless, by the exercise of its own will, to resist or control the propensity. And unless it finds an authoritative and sane guardian and controller in the Supreme Court—unless this Court has itself, by chance, escaped this widely spread moral imbecility of vicious type, there seems to be no cure for the disease, nor end to its wickedness. And Philadelphia must still continue to stand, as she now does, alone, among all the cities of the old free States, in the exercise of this most infamous system of class persecution.

When Lear cries out "Let them anatomise Regan; see what breeds about her heart," we are made to perceive that his mind was not so wholly absorbed in his wrongs as to prevent it from speculating, in a wild way, on their cause: a touch of nature suggesting that any statement of wrongs which does not enter into the causes and conditions that made their commission possible, is imperfect. And to the question constantly recurring: What is it that has caused the people of Philadelphia thus to stand apart from other northern and western free cities, in the disposition to persecute negroes? the true answer seems to be this: Philadelphia once owned more slaves than any other northern city, with the possible exception of New York; she retains a greater number of colored people now, in proportion to her white population, than any other such city, with the accidental exception of New Bedford,* when emancipation took place the process was left incomplete, and of all cities, north or south, she most fears amalgamation.

The evils of slavery are in proportion to its density. In South Carolina, which is the part of the United States where it was most dense, these evils, especially in their effect on the Whites, were more distinct and apparent than in any other State. The South Carolinians were the most despotic of our slave owners, and they were the first to secede in order to remain such undisturbed. But great as were these evils in our slave States, where the Whites always outnumbered the Blacks, they were infinitely greater in the West Indies, and especially in St. Domingo, where the Blacks, in a much greater degree, outnumbered the Whites. The most comprehensive evidence of this is to be found in the fact that, in the United States there was a natural increase in the slave population, while in the West Indies the reverse was the case, to a remarkable degree. A slave, when landed in the United States, always found here at least two Whites to one Black; for before the introduction of the cotton gin, which was not until after the abolition of the slave trade, the temptation was not great to drive plantation work, or to increase the number of slaves. He came at once into such multiplied contact with Whites that, though he was taught nothing, he learnt much. His African superstitions soon died out, or became greatly diluted; camp meeting exercises took their place; his games and dances were assimilated to those of white people, and his spontaneous songs, unlike those of the St. Domingo negroes, which mostly relate to eating, satire and venery, early be-

* According to the census of 1860, the proportion of the colored to the white population in the cities named below, was as follows:

Boston, ...	1 colored to $77\frac{3}{5}$	white.
New York, ...	1 " " $63\frac{1}{2}$	"
Philadelphia, ...	1 " " $24\frac{1}{2}$	"

In New Bedford, at the same census, the proportion was found to be one colored to $13\frac{1}{2}$ white. The comparatively large number of colored people in that city is said to be due to the special kindness with which runaway slaves were received there, and to the fact that it afforded them a somewhat safe place of refuge, because it was out of the main line of travel.

came emotional and religious.* The first tincture of Christianity which West India slaves received, was communicated to them by slaves from the United States. When Dr. Coke landed in St. Eustatia, in 1788, he found, as his Journal says, that "the Lord had raised up lately a negro slave named Harry, brought here from the continent to prepare our way." The Baptists, now the great sect of Jamaica, owe their origin there to George Lisle, a slave preacher, who was taken thither from Georgia, by his tory master, at the evacuation of Savannah by the British in 1782.

But a cargo of slaves, on being landed in French St. Domingo, found there, towards the last days of the colony, nearly twenty of their own to one of the white race. They were at once herded with the former. As their immediate overseers were mostly creole Blacks, many of them rarely, except at a distance, saw white people, of whom there were barely enough to conduct the business of the colony. The number of doctors was insufficient. The planters depended on importation rather than personal care to keep up their stock of slaves. This stock was often changed, in consequence of its being worked up. There was a constant renewal of the savage element by slave ships. The new slaves always found in St. Domingo the customs and superstitions they had left in Africa. They added freshness to them, and then all went on together, as nearly as possible, in the old African way. In fact, it might almost have seemed, had it been possible, as if parts of French St. Domingo had been covered with African sod, bearing with it its native life and growth, little disturbed by

* Our Southern negro English, uncouth as it sounds, is pure compared to that of the British Islands; and in the French West Indies and Hayti, the divergence between the creole *patois* and French is still wider. The negroes actually impressed the use of their dialect deeply upon the Whites, and to this day it is the colloquial language of all classes, whether educated or not, in these islands. The same negro ascendancy can be traced in their amusements. The *Bamboula* and the *Calenda* of the French islands and Hayti, and certain similar dances in Cuba, are, somewhat modified and restrained, still favorites with the white people. They are all African in their origin, and their type is lasciviousness. In the British islands these dances have in a great degree given way before the teachings of the Baptist, Methodist and Moravian missionaries.

the transfer. Hence *vaudouxism*, or serpent-worship went on, in full vigor, in spite of law and the police, and, to some extent, cannibalism, up to the very moment when the colony was suddenly blown to atoms by the over-generation of its own wickedness,—the Whites, who worked it, being thereby destroyed, or scattered to distant lands, with all their means and appliances of civilization. And as the Blacks, who remained in possession, shut the door against the return of the Whites, from fear of returning slavery, and yet keep it shut, in consequence of a still remaining vague jealousy, thus barring out foreign improvements, it is not surprising that the superstitious and barbarous usages of St. Domingo at this day prevail, to no small degree, in Hayti. The towns around the coast, where a few white merchants and the educated mulattoes reside, may be considered as tufts of civilization, and the savage traits inseparable from dense slavery have been a good deal softened down among the country people. But we might as reasonably expect to find an advanced state of civilization in the neighborhood of the Portuguese trading settlements on the west coast of Africa as in the interior of Hayti. For want of a proper knowledge of these facts, the non-civilization of Hayti has always been a thorn in the side of abolitionists, and from the same cause, the North generally, during the first half of the late war, was constantly looking for a second edition of the "Horrors of St. Domingo" in the South. But the freedmen of the South have no more in common with the insurrectionary slaves of 1791, in St. Domingo, than any other humanized people have with savages. It is fair to admit that this superior moral and physical condition of our southern Blacks over those of St. Domingo is due, in some degree, to difference of race in the masters. The descendants of French Protestants, English Wesleyans and Baptists, and Austrian Salzburgers, and even those resulting from a cross between Cavaliers and convict-servants, were doubtless less inhuman slave-masters than the progeny of buccaneers and *flibustiers*. Still the main difference arose from different degrees of density in slavery. Our southern slaves had the best opportunities to learn by looking on. And the most valuable trait in the negro, and that which will most avail to his salvation as a race, is that, whenever he is within reach of civilization, he silently puts forth a tendril and clasps it.

On the Whites, the most curious effect of dense slavery is that of destroying, or greatly impairing the power of moral vision in all matters relating to Blacks. In this respect, the trial for murder of the Hon. Arthur Hodge, planter and member of His Majesty's Council in the island of Tortola, and there hanged, in 1811, is a psychological study. Along through the years including 1805 and 1808, this gentleman, by cart-whipping at "short quarters," by pouring boiling water down the throat, by burning with hot irons and by dipping in coppers of scalding water, murdered eight of his slaves and one freeman. Tortola is twelve miles long by four broad and at the time in question contained about 6000 inhabitants. These murders were well known to the slave population, when committed, and as testimony afterwards proved, to many of the Whites. But Hodge was not brought to trial till 1811, and then formal complaint against him only reached his brother magistrates through a family quarrel about property. John M'Donough declined to serve on the jury because "the case would make the negroes saucy." Stephen M'Keough, a planter and an important witness, who saw some of these cases of flogging which ended in death, described Mr. Hodge as "a good man, but comical, because he had bad slaves." Both the Attorney General and the presiding Judge, apparently functionaries from England, thought it necessary to go into a set argument to show that killing negro slaves was really murder, and the jury, under the charge, brought Hodge in guilty, but recommended him to mercy. Here was moral blindness produced by an atmosphere of slavery which can only find its physical counterpart in the eyeless fishes bred in the dark waters of the Kentucky cave. Probably no case could be found in our Southern States equal to this in enormity of crime and corresponding absence of moral vision in respect to it, though that of Mrs. Abrahams, of Virginia, with her four murders, and the alacrity with which "all the Richmond lawyers" volunteered in her defence may approach it.

In Pennsylvania the slaves were never more than a sprinkling compared to the free population, slavery never appeared in these dark colors, and it was early declared to be prospectively abolished. And yet this old, unmistakable characteristic of the slaveholder—defect of moral vision where the black man is concerned, is to this day a distinct feature of our society. We are still unable to see clearly the wickedness of denying him the vote and expelling him from the cars; and the same spirit of outrage and murder, which now shocks us by the terrible energy with which it moves the late slaveholders against the freedmen, is at this moment acting in a small, feeble, mean way within ourselves against our own colored population. The difference is one of degree, not of kind. Thus, eighty-six years after the passage of the act for the gradual emancipation of the slaves of Pennsylvania, life enough remains in the old institution, long since supposed extinct, still to disturb the peace of society.

Our fathers made two great mistakes in this matter. First, the process of extinction was to be gradual, which was as if one, instead of a bullet, should give a dose of slow poison to a mad dog and then let him run; and next, it was not only gradual but incomplete. The chain of the slave was broken but not taken off; and any degree of civil disability under which an emancipated slave is left, is just so much slavery left. It not only restrains his movements both of progress and self-defence, but it keeps alive the spirit of oppression in the "master race" as air keeps alive flame. By a natural law, whatever of the slave is left in one race will, while it lasts, always tempt into exercise and encounter a corresponding amount of the slave master in the other. So long as the law degrades a man, his neighbor will degrade him. Whoever can call to mind a celebration of our day of Independence in Philadelphia five and thirty years ago, may remember that the part of the day's exercises which the boys took upon themselves was to stone and club colored people out of Independence Square, because "niggers had nothing to do with the Fourth of July." The fathers of these boys looked on with placid satisfaction, cheerfully and hopefully remarking to each other, how well their sons were learning to perform the duties of free American citizens. Twenty years later and a change might be seen. Colored people—place and occasion the same—were allowed to carry water about among the crowd, without meeting other insult from the thirsty than words of good-natured contempt. This was an improvement. Those whom we formerly drove forth with blows and curses, we had now learned to utilize. Twelve more years go by, and on the Fourth of July we were enlisting our able bodied colored men to fight for us. But we still were mindful of what was due to ourselves, as belonging to the superior race, and when they came back to us, wounded in our defence, we carefully restricted their wives and sisters to the front platform of the cars, when they visited their husbands and brothers at the hospitals. And now to-day, out of sixteen Philadelphia generals and colonels, most of whom are believed to have seen some service in the field, three vote in favor of permitting these returned colored veterans actually to join in the celebration of our great National Anniversary. This is progress, but it is slow, and the causes of the obstruction to it must be sought in the incomplete emancipation of 1780.

But another cause which gives Philadelphia a bad eminence in respect to the treatment of colored people, is the comparatively large numbers of them which she possesses over other northern cities, with the one exception above noted; and this cause seems simply to connect with and form part of another—the fear of amalgamation. This fear greatly disturbs a large portion of our white population. In discussing the car question, an opponent of admission at once urges that it will be a stepping stone to amalgamation. The suggestion that seven disabled colored soldiers might safely be allowed equal privileges in a military hospital with 160 white soldiers, is put aside with the remark that such a rule would countenance amalgamation. The matron, with downcast eyes and timid horror, intimates this objection to the reception, into the same Orphan Home, of little white and colored children, mostly between the ages of four and ten. All this sounds very illogical. Hitherto, there has been little amalgamation of the two races at the North, and as the colored people never make advances to the Whites, that little cannot be increased until the Whites make advances to them. When is this to begin? Let each one answer this question individually. This matter, in its negative aspect, rests entirely within the control of the white population.

The broad distinction, so often pointed out, between political and social equality, is still by many of our people persistently confounded, and perhaps it may be necessary to state it once more. Political equality everybody has the present or prospective right to demand—social equality nobody; for the barrier which separates the two is made up of private door-steps. Each of these, its owner has absolutely at his own command, and no man has a right to prescribe, even by implication, whom he shall permit, or forbid, to pass it. It is not an open question.

But supposing the relations, so long sustained at the North, between the two races, and which the Blacks do not complain of, when unaccompanied with wrongs, were suddenly to cease; and everywhere, North and South, on both sides, impelled by an irrepressible orgasm, they should rush together. There are, in round numbers, 26,000,000 of white and 4,000,000 of colored people in the United States; and after every Black had found a White, there would remain 22,000,000 of Whites still unmated. These, by necessity, would carry on the pure white population, and they might safely be left, without help, to sustain themselves in the struggle of race, against the 8,000,000 of amalgamationists. But here it is asserted, they will receive aid from a distinct source. According to the theory of Doctors Nott and Cartwright, the mixed race rapidly decays, and after three generations dies out. This theory is accepted by those who fear amalgamation, and is often quoted by them, as an argument against the theory of equal rights. They also hate negroes and would be glad to see their numbers less. But pure-blooded negroes, it is generally conceded, possess great vitality of race and are killed off with difficulty. This difficulty, it seems, can be overcome by amalgamation. By this process, in one generation, all these negroes become mulattoes, and this once accomplished, the whole African race is in a fair way to disappear from the land. These advocates for pure white blood have been defeating their own purpose. Let them reverse their policy and encourage, for a time, the amalgamation they have hitherto opposed, and, with patience, they can have a white man's government yet.

This proposition is less extravagant than are these insane and wicked fears of impending amalgamation ;—wicked, because they are made the excuse, by the race that has the entire preventive control of the matter, for maltreating colored people and denying them rights which are accorded, without dispute, to every other man and woman in the country.

But these people will never come to such an end as this ; and if it is true that amalgamation, here, leads towards it, then here, to any considerable extent, it will never take place. They were never made the valuable element of our population, which they are, simply to die out. The greater part of the work which has yet been done on a large portion of this continent has been done by them, and apparently they ever will be, as they ever have been, absolutely essential to its full development.

This statement does not imply that the slave trade and slavery were right or necessary. The sin was not in the bringing of Africans to America, but in the manner of bringing them. God has established His own fixed laws to govern the movements of peoples, but He permits men to carry them out according to their will. Had men willed to be just and humane, they could have induced Africans to come to this continent as free emigrants ; but they were selfish and wicked, and therefore forced them to come as slaves. Slavery has been, and is, destroying itself everywhere ; and in this country, the great system of free labor and equal rights which prevails, without qualification, in some of the Northern States, is now being offered, and in spite of all opposition will soon be applied, to every State, north and south. It is not probable that it will stop there. It is believed that the same system is destined, in time, to be extended into our tropics. The so-called Anglo-Saxon race in England colonizes ; in the United States it expands. Mr. Disraeli lately pronounced England more an Asiatic than a European power ; and the day may come when we shall be as much a power of South America as we now are of North America. We have a means to facilitate future extension into the tropics in an element of our home population, suited to them, which England never possessed in hers ; and after this has been received into our body politic, and is thus enabled to develop its powers, it is not easy to resist the conclusion that its destiny is to carry our civilization into these latitudes. The feeble and imperfect nationalities lying to the south of us are apparently but provisional. They are waiting a better system than their own, and higher powers than they possess, to apply it. The time is likely to come when their ability to furnish the products peculiar to their soil will fall short of the wants of the civilized world without; and should this be the case, it will stimulate us to carry thither our enterprise, and with it our laws and institutions. This has been the process by which they have been carried into California, by Whites alone—gold being the lure; but to places farther south our people of color, from their special climatic fitness for it, must assist in being their vehicle; and the two races must go towards the tropics, if at all, together. The African will never leave this country, but he may, in the legitimate pursuit of his own interests and happiness, assist in its expansion beyond its present limits; and, soon or late, should the practical assertion of our "Monroe Doctrine" make it necessary for us to carry our arms into tropical latitudes, the late war has shown us where to find soldiers. These are speculations, but it would be hard to show that they are without some groundwork of probable reality in the future. Meantime it is well to feel assured that these people are here for the good, and not the evil of both races, and that interest as well as justice demands that every right and privilege which we possess should be freely and at once extended to them. Let us trust God to do His own justice, not fearing that harm will come of it unless we interpose with our injustice; and let us no longer believe that if we do what is right and humane as a people to-day, we shall be punished for it tomorrow; for this is practical atheism.

www.ingramcontent.com/pod-product-compliance
Lightning Source LLC
La Vergne TN
LVHW011140110826
845150LV00008B/2423